LOOKING AT CHRISTIANITY

Jesus and Mary

GRAHAM OWEN and ALISON SEAMAN

WAYLAND

Festivals
Jesus and Mary
Special Occasions
Worship

Editors: Carron Brown and Ruth Raudsepp
Series consultant: Alison Seaman
Designer and typesetter: Jean Wheeler
Cover designer: Steve Wheele Design
Picture researcher: Gina Brown

First published in 1998 by Wayland Publishers Ltd,
61 Western Road, Hove, East Sussex, BN3 1JD

British Library Cataloguing in Publication Data
Seaman, Alison
Jesus and Mary. – (Looking at Christianity)
1. Jesus Christ – Biography – Juvenile literature
2. Jesus Christ – Teachings – Juvenile literature
3. Mary, Mother of Jesus Christ – Biography – Juvenile literature
I. Title II. Owen, Graham
232.9'01

ISBN 0 7502 2241 7

Picture acknowledgements
Andes Press Agency 16 (Carlos Reyes-Manzo); Audio Visual Productions UK 27; Collections 13 (Liba
Taylor); Getty Images 4 (Stuart Cohen), 6 (Charles Thatcher), 8 (Poulides/Thatcher); Sally and Richard
Greenhill 12; Sonia Halliday 11, 18, 24 (Jane Taylor); Robert Harding 5 (Walter Rawlings), 9 (Walter
Rawlings); McCrimmons Publishing 19 (Gerald Coates); Topham Picturepoint 10; Visual Arts Library
7, 22; Wayland Picture Library 14 (National Gallery), 15, 17 (Dorothy Hill), 20 (Zul Mukhida), 21
(Imogen Stuart), 23 (Tim Woodcock), 25 (Rupert Horrox), 26 (Rupert Horrox).

Cover photo by Danny Allmark.

Printed and bound by EuroGrafica S.p.A., Italy

232
D

Contents

All religious words are explained in the glossary.

The wonder of life

Here is Peter with his mother.

Peter has just been born. His mother wonders what his future will be.

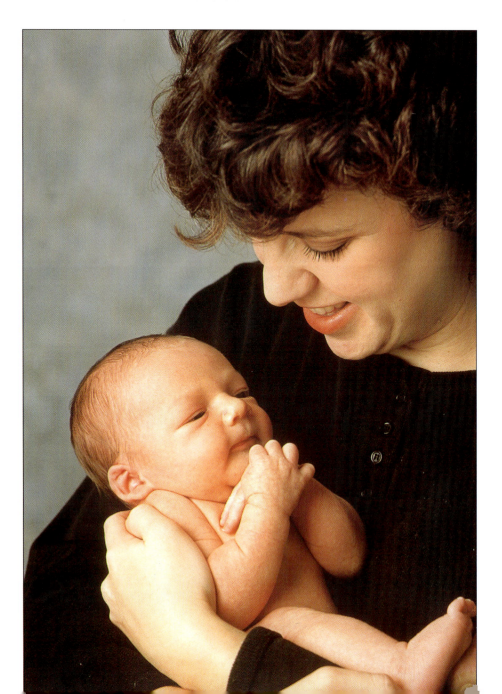

Many years ago, Mary had a baby boy called Jesus.

Just like Peter's mother, Mary wondered what Jesus' future would be like. You can read about Jesus and his mother Mary in the Bible.

We are all different but we are all special people.

Christians believe that God knows everyone and has important work for each person to do.

God chose Mary to care for Jesus.

Mary is a very special person for Christians because she was chosen by God to do this.

Mary has a baby

Angela is going to have a baby.

She is excited about being a mother. Angela wonders what her baby will be like. She knows that looking after a baby is hard work. She wonders how she will cope with her new child.

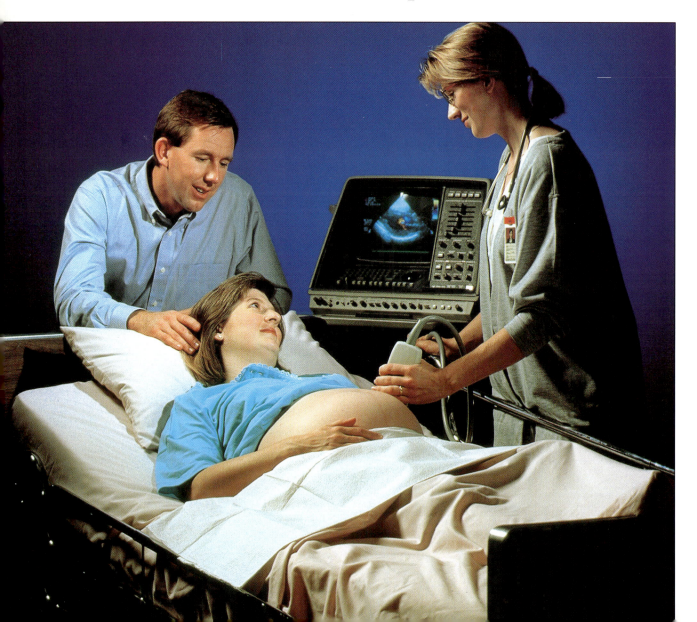

Mary was surprised when she found she was going to have a baby.

Christians read in the Bible that God sent an angel to see Mary. The angel carried an important message from God. He told Mary that she was going to be the mother of Jesus.

This picture shows some of Jesus' ancestors.

Christians believe that God promised to send His son Jesus into the world. He would be the new leader that had been written about in the Bible.

Jesus was born in a stable.

Mary and her husband Joseph went on a journey just before Jesus was born. They could not find anywhere to stay, so Jesus was born in a stable. Mary and Joseph cared for him and made sure he was safe.

Jesus' early life

Jesus grew up with his brothers and sisters.

Even though he was born into an ordinary family, Jesus was a special person whose life would affect many people throughout history.

Jesus lived in a country we now call Israel.

Jesus' family was Jewish. He learned all about the history and beliefs of the Jewish people. Jesus decided that he wanted to become a teacher.

Jesus is baptised

As he grew up, Jesus knew he had a special job to do.

His cousin John recognised that Jesus was the Son of God. He agreed to baptise him. Then Jesus travelled around the country teaching and preaching about God.

This picture shows a Christian baptism in Jamaica.

Christians around the world continue to welcome people into God's family by baptising them. People can be baptised at any age, from tiny babies to grown ups.

Jesus the teacher

Jesus taught that God loves and cares for everyone.

He also helped people who were in need and healed people who were sick. The teachings of Jesus are still important for Christians today.

Christians of all ages learn from each other.

Children and adults read the Bible together and learn more about God. They know there is always something new to think about.

The Bible tells of many different events in the life of Jesus.

Sometimes Mary was with him and she encouraged others to trust him. In this picture, Jesus and his mother go to a wedding. The wine ran out and Jesus turned the jugs of water into wine.

Jesus' life in danger

Not everybody agreed with Jesus.

Some people hated him so much they wanted to get rid of him. In this wood carving, Jesus is accused of being a dangerous trouble maker. These men have made him their prisoner.

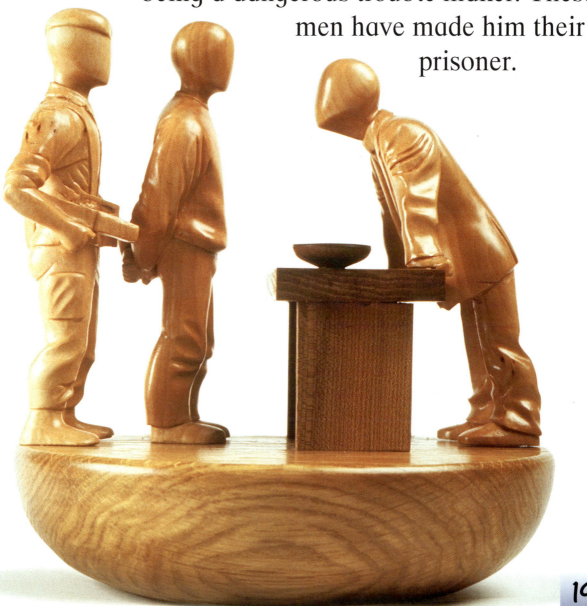

Jesus knew that his life was in danger.

He was sentenced to death and he was forced to wear a crown of thorns on his head. This reminds Christians that Jesus had to suffer a lot of pain.

The end of the story?

Mary was with Jesus when he died.

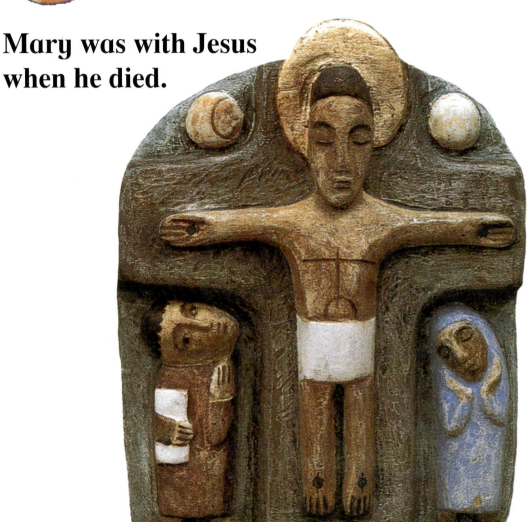

Jesus' hands and feet were nailed to a large cross and he was left there to die. Mary thought she would never see him again, but still she trusted in God. Christians know this is a very sad story. But it does not end here.

The hope of new life

This church window shows Jesus coming to life again.

The Bible tells that after three days Jesus rose from the dead. His mother and his friends were able to see him when he visited them.

These children are excited when their bulbs produce flowers in the spring.

In the same way, the story of Jesus helps Christians to know that there is always hope of new life.

Remembering Jesus and Mary

When Christians meet together they feel that Jesus is still with them.

Throughout the world, Christians remember Jesus when they worship together. They think about his life and learn from his teachings.

Anabelle and Jairaj have found the banner in their church showing a picture of Mary.

She inspires them to be faithful and trusting even in times of difficulty, and to love and care for their friends and family.

CHRIST ✠ CHURCH
SHOOTERS ✠ HILL

25

Billy looks at his icon of Jesus and Mary.

Jesus and Mary help Billy to feel closer to God. He believes that God will care for him throughout his life and forgive him when he does something wrong.

Heaven

This picture shows an artist's idea of heaven.

Christians hope that one day they will be in heaven with Jesus and his mother Mary. What do you think heaven might be like?

Notes for teachers

About the pictures

The images used in this series are in many respects as important as the text. The historical nature of the subject requires that we use illustrations and photographs as well as actors' representations to enliven the text for children. The images will provide stimuli for discussion and enable children to engage imaginatively with the subject matter.

pp 4–5 All children will have some experience of the excitement and wonder associated with new life – the birth of a brother or sister, pets having babies, observing new life in nature. The story of the birth of Jesus from Mary's point of view can be explored through the children's own experience.

pp6–7 Christians believe that all people have a vocation – a role in life that is special for them and through which they make a unique contribution in the world. While this is fulfilled by Christians in many different ways, it is believed that Mary's vocation was to be the mother of Jesus. Although Mary was a mother like any other, she had a significant role to play in the Christian story.

pp 8–9 The anticipation of the birth of a new baby is shown in this picture where the mother and father see their baby through the marvel of modern technology. In the Bible, the news of Mary's pregnancy is told in the story known as the Annunciation – the Angel Gabriel announced to Mary that she was to be the mother of Jesus. This has been a favourite subject for artists and is often depicted on Christmas cards.

pp 10–11 Christians believe that Jesus was the Messiah promised in the Jewish scriptures. The picture on page 10 is an illustration of his family tree. It is depicted in this way to show his royal ancestry. For Christians, the wonder of Jesus' birth is that God became human and was born into an ordinary family. Jesus was born, not into a cosy comfortable home, but in a stable, away from friends and family and in hostile circumstances. Throughout his life, Jesus was associated with the poor and disadvantaged. The circumstances of his birth are the first of many examples of this. For Christians around the world and throughout the ages, this has been a source of comfort and inspiration.

pp 12–13 In the Bible, there is very little information about Jesus' early life. It is known that as a Jew, Jesus would have learned from the scriptures the history and practices of the Jewish people. It is still significant for Jewish children today to learn and maintain this tradition . One event in Jesus' early life is recounted in Luke's Gospel (2:41–52), when he travelled to Jerusalem with his parents for Passover. He disappeared and his parents found him, sometime later, with a group of Rabbis in the temple.

pp 14–15 Jesus' cousin John baptised people as a sign of forgiveness for their sins and Jesus asked John to baptise him in the River Jordan. In the Bible, Christians read that God was present at this baptism. In the painting on page 14, the artist shows this by painting a dove hovering over the head of Jesus. For Christians, baptism marks the admission of a person into the faith; the forgiveness of sins and the receiving of the Holy Spirit.

pp 16–17 Jesus became a well known teacher often addressing large numbers of people. His message focused on the love of God for everyone and he often used stories to illustrate this. For Christians throughout the world, learning about the faith is a lifelong process. All ages learn from each other in both formal and informal settings.

p 18 During the period of Jesus' ministry, the Bible has few references to Mary, but one event which is recorded in detail, is referred to as the Wedding at Cana (see John 2:1–11). This was the setting for Jesus' first miracle when he changed water into wine. There are various ways of looking at the miracles of Jesus, and for many Christians it is their symbolic meaning that is important. For the Gospel writers, the Jewish Scriptures and future events in Jesus' life influenced the way the stories are told.

p 19 Jesus was seen by many at the time as a revolutionary. He challenged the accepted norms of society and his claim to be the Son of God was seen by many of his contemporaries as heretical. This led to his trial and subsequent sentence to death. The Gospels record that Jesus' enemies trapped him and forced him to stand trial on false charges.

p 20 Christians believe that through the agony of his death, Jesus identifies with human pain and suffering. Moreover, his willingness to obey God's will, by dying in this way, is seen by Christians as the ultimate sacrifice. During the Roman occupation, crucifixion was the common form of execution for convicted criminals. Mary is said to have witnessed her son's death. This horrific event is challenging for both adults and children, but remains central to understanding the Christian story, that Jesus died to fulfil God's promise to save humankind. Although this is a difficult subject to discuss with young children, the Christian story is incomplete without it

pp 21 Christians identify with the anguish felt by Mary as she watched her son die on the cross. Her trust and faith in God inspires Christian commitment. Stemming from this, within some Christian traditions Mary is the most revered of all the saints.

pp 22–3 The death of Jesus is only one part of the Christian story. We read in the Bible that Jesus was raised from the dead, and so the cross becomes the hope of new life. The cross is the universal symbol for all Christians. The gospel accounts of the resurrection are interpreted in different ways, but belief in life after death is central to Christian faith. For young children the events of the Easter story are expressed well through observations of the natural world.

pp 24–5 The events in the life of Jesus and Mary recounted in this book took place a long time ago. Christians believe, however, that Jesus is a powerful force in their lives today. His memory is kept alive through prayer, the festivals of the Christian Church and in worship. In some traditions, Mary is venerated as an inspiration to faith, trust and obedience.

pp 26– 7 Jesus and Mary are not only significant role models for Christians today, but also a source of love and care. Central to Christian faith is the understanding that God came into the world as Jesus and lives on as a life giving spirit. Christians hold many different views about heaven, but for all it represents a new life closer to God.

Glossary

angel A messenger from God

banner A kind of flag usually made of cloth, showing Christian pictures.

baptised When people are baptised they become Christians.

baptism The service that welcomes people into the Christian family.

Bible The most important book for all Christians.

Christians People who follow the teachings of Jesus Christ.

cross Jesus was put to death on a cross. It has become the symbol of hope for all Christians.

Heaven The place where Christians hope they will be after they die.

icon A special kind of picture of Jesus or one of the saints.

worship When Christians praise God together.

Books to read

Books for children

A Child's Book of Prayer in Art by Sister Wendy Beckett (Dorling Kindersley, 1995)

My Christian Life by Alison Seaman (Wayland, 1996)

The Beginner's Bible by Karyn Henley (Kingsway Publications, 1989)

Books for teachers

A Gift to the Child, RE in the Primary School by Michael Grimmitt, Julie Grove, John Hull, Louise Spencer (Simon Schuster) Teachers' Source Book

Audio-visual materials

Channel 4 Animated Bible stories, available from Channel 4 publications

Inspire – poster pack, (Diocese of Winchester and Salisbury, 1996)

Index